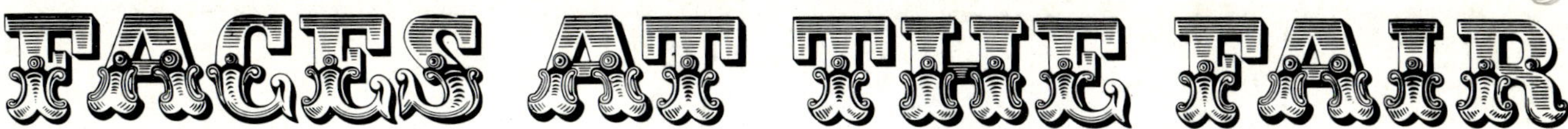

FACES AT THE FAIR

A photographic essay on
the 'Ould Lammas Fair'
at Ballycastle, Co Antrim
by
Stanley Matchett

Blackstaff Press Limited

THE FRUIT SHOP
CHURCH ARMY
Cushendall
A2
Harbour
ROAD

'At the Oul' Lammas Fair boy,
were you ever there,
at the Oul' Lammas Fair at
Ballycastle-o.
Did you trate your Mary Ann
To Dulse and Yella-man
At the Oul' Lammas Fair at
Ballycastle-o?'

The Diamond

INTRODUCTION

The Lammas Fair, a two-day event, which takes its name from the Anglo-Saxon 'loaf mass' or 'feast of the first fruits', is now nearing its 400th birthday. Why it has survived other Irish fairs is a mystery. Perhaps it is the Dulse and the Yellow Man they've heard so much about, or perhaps the thriftiness of the Antrim folk has assured the fair's reputation as a place for a good bargain.

Ballycastle is a little seaside town of 3,000 people in North Antrim, surrounded by some of the most spectacular coastal scenery in the British Isles. Every year, on the last Tuesday in August, the hawkers, fortune tellers, wheelers and dealers set up shop in the Diamond there, ready and waiting for the host of visitors — some 40,000 per day — who descend on the town at fair-time. Multicoloured stalls are everywhere, two hundred of them spilling into the surrounding streets, selling everything from mousetraps to mangles, brollies, ballpoints, cheap shirts and flowery dresses. The hotels, pubs and restaurants do a roaring trade. Everyone is eager to savour the free-'n-easy carnival atmosphere. Some carry their drinks to the pub door and watch the girls go by, while the tables in the back yard attract the open air drinkers — all a far cry from the days when the fair was held on the ramparts of Dunanynie Castle, a stronghold of the McDonnells, when boatloads from the Isle of Islay made the 26 mile journey by sailboat.

Coachloads of bargain hunters jostle round the stalls, lured by the twin delights of Dulse — packets of chewy dried seaweed — and Yella-man — the home made sticky rock which looks like pale gold toffee. The coloured vendors with their turbans and soft black eyes are there, bringing the mysterious Orient to the neat wee town on the edge of the grey Atlantic. They peddle their wares — cheesecloth shirts and dresses, and haberdashery as alluring and brilliant as a heap of liquorice allsorts.

As the day wears on, the stalls start to come down. A quietness creeps over the crowd. A police car noses its way gently through the thinning throng. A tipsy gent picks his steps carefully, staggering a little as he makes his way slowly down the main street. At the Gospel stall the sandwich board man is still there. 'Woe to the bloody city that all full of lies', his back view proclaims, as he hands out religious tracts to people too tired and laden to read them. He is always one of the first to arrive and the last to leave. As the darkness comes in over the mountains and the sea, the gaiety of the day carries on in pubs and at dances. The fair is all things to all people, and a traditional link with past and happier times.

Stanley Matchett

Jaunting

Food for the body

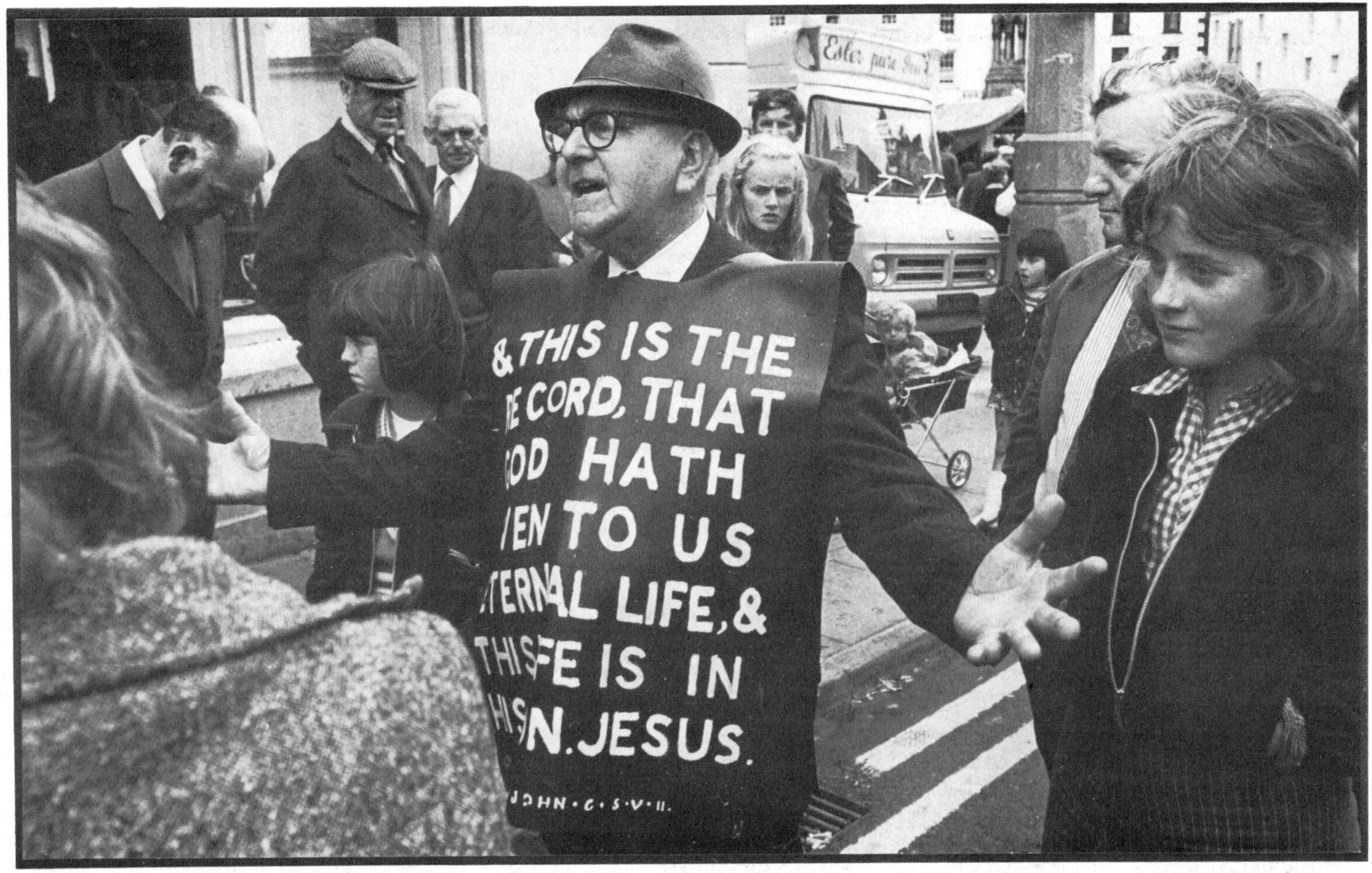

Food for the soul

Looking

Discovering

Directing

The mysterious East

e music maker

The brassware boy

The women who know what they want

'he girls who know what they like

'Come 'ere boy!'

'Come along folks!'

Crash goes a slab of Yellow Man,
– the recipe is a well kept secret

Sold! A transistor from Tokyo goes to the highest bidder

. . . Down goes the Dulse,
dried seaweed with a salty tang

Odd antiques

Memories

. . . *And modern momentos*

Boots . . .

. . . and saddles

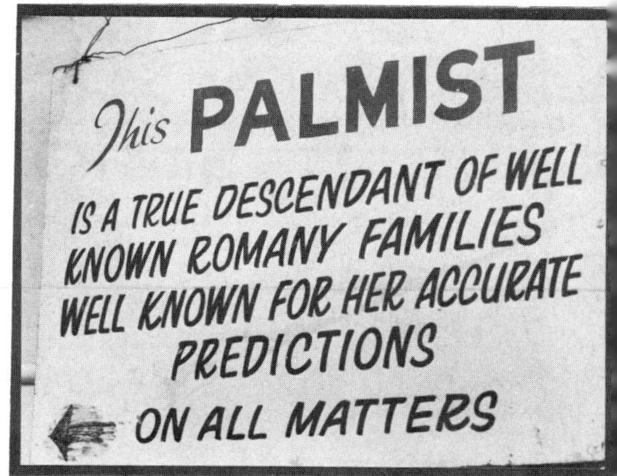

. . . and fortunes told

Quiet thoughts

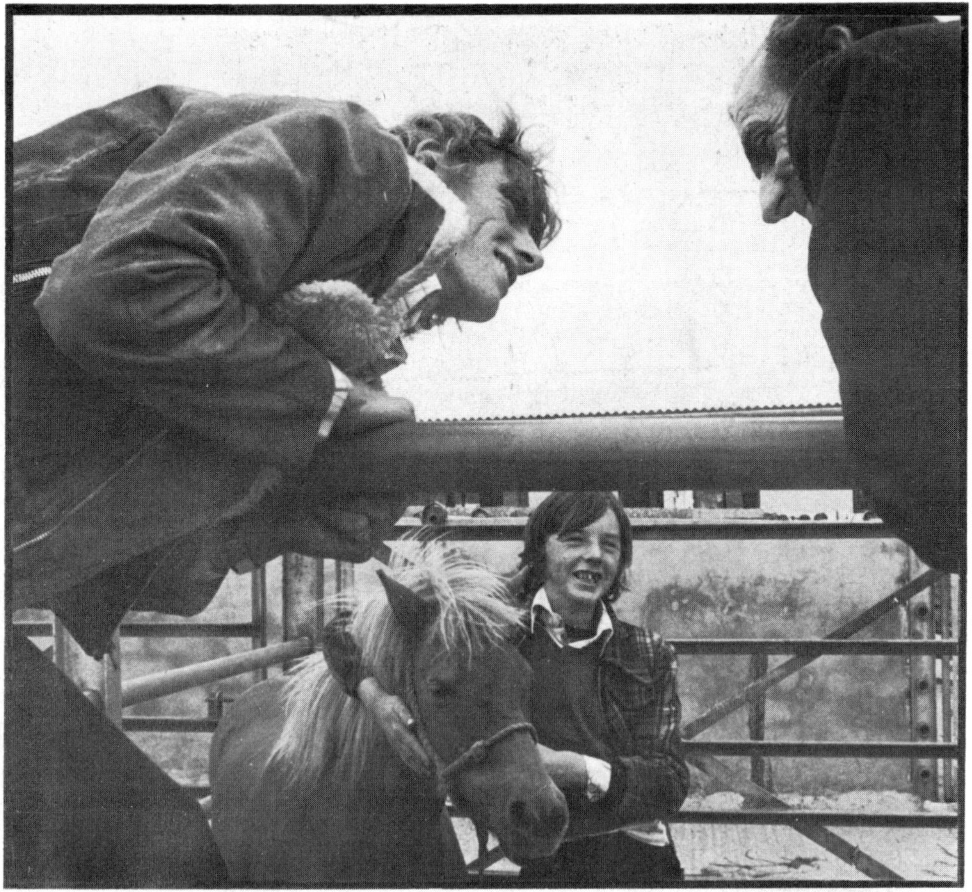

and paddock laughs

'Time Please' to watch the crowds pass by

. . . with their bargains of the day

A working lunch for some

A working tool for others

Patient ponies

A big question for a small child

Shells,

and skirts

and suits

. . . and games with goldfish bowls

Picture palace

Plants and panes

The bright day is done

Published by Blackstaff Press Limited, 16 Donegall Square South, Belfast BT1 5JF

SBN 85640 094 7

Printed by Belfast Litho Printers Limited, Belfast.